These Things Will They Do Unto You

Exposing the Devil in Church Conflict

For information address:
J2B Publishing LLC
4251 Columbia Park Road
Pomfret, MD 20675
www.J2BLLC.com

Printed and bound in the United States of America.

This book is set in Garamond.

ISBN: 978-1-948747-46-2

These Things Will They Do Unto You

Exposing the Devil in Church Conflict

Randy and Cheryl Heddings

J2B PUBLISHING

Forward

Reverend James B. Cook, Jr.

When I first heard about Job's Place from Rev. Dr. Thomas Randy Heddings, I was overwhelmed by the heart warming, vibrant, and energized Hand of the Holy Spirit in Bro. Randy's life. When I was asked to be a part of this ministry I was deeply moved and became one of awe, exceeding joy, and ever lasting commitment to the work of helping pastors who are in need of a place to recuperate, in body, soul and spirit.

King David in his writing of the Psalms states that he needed his joy of salvation restored, and he desired to be upheld by the free Spirit of God. Even a man, like David, being ones with God's own heart needed the restoring and refreshing of the Holy Spirit in able to do God's will in his life.

I am so honored to be a friend and prayer warrior of Pastor Randy, who is a mighty man of God. As the Associate Pastor, at Pathway Baptist Church, where Randy serves as Pastor, I see God working in the life of

Job's Place and in the personal life and ministry of Pastor Randy and his wife Cheryl (a Minister herself), and their daughter Jessica.

I just want to thank God for His Handy work in this ministry and am looking forward to see His mighty works of faith as Job's Place takes on a life of Restoring Pastors to be able to do His Will in their lives as He prepares them for 4 further work in the ministry of spreading the Gospel of Jesus Christ.

As you read this book, I pray that you will open your mind and heart to what is being said. May you receive and enjoy the comfort and peace that is to be found within the covers of this book written by Pastor Randy. Glory to God, Our Father and Creator, His Son Jesus, our Lord and Savior, and the Holy Spirit. Our comforter who leads us in Spirit and in Truth.

Dedication

You will see, by the title of this book that it is taken from a part of John 16:3. John 16:2 show Jesus speaking to His disciples about what will come in later years. He is speaking in prophecy at this point but is indeed addressing a situation that is now almost at epidemic proportion today. The Word of God is being rejected in the written form and in the Living Word form. The Logos and Rhema word are both being swallowed up in the churches today through compromise. Ministers are being discharged from churches all around the world today because people think they have God figured out and are doing Him a service by running ministers off from "their" church. I am convinced they are not doing God a favor but they are doing the minister a favor by releasing them.

To those ministers, male or female, Pastor, Prophet, Evangelist, Teacher or Apostle, Missionary or whatever title you might have, we dedicate this book to you. This book is for those faithful warriors that have stood in times of battle and went on about the ministry keeping Jesus first, realizing that Jesus is their first Love.

For the minister's families that have stood by their spouses during the toughest and perhaps the cruelest parts of the life of ministry, we appreciate you.

To those that have been fortunate enough to have never been through a church crisis in their ministry, we dedicate this book in hopes that when you hear of someone in a hurtful situation you will be better equipped to inform them of what is going to happen next and stand with them in prayer against those things.

Finally, to all ministers that will eventually go through these times as the close of the world as we know it begins to come to us.

May God bestow His wisdom upon you as you read this book we pray in Jesus' Holy Name, Amen.

Table of Contents

Introduction

John 16:2-3: *"for you will be expelled from the synagogues, and the time is coming when those who kill you will think they are doing God a service. This is because they have never known me or the Father."*

There have been times in the ministry that I have wondered what in the world was going on. How in the world could Christians act the way they act and do the things they do? Perhaps, somewhere along the way in your ministry you could relate to this scripture in your life or perhaps it will give you encouragement after going through a tough time in the ministry.

The Lord writes to us in His word about how people would be as the last times approach. This is a great scripture that reveals to us the truth about what the Apostle Paul wrote to young Timothy. He writes that there would be those that turn to their own desires and there are those that will have a form of godliness but deny the power thereof.

God places ministers into the presence of these people to attempt to bring them into the fold where He is and allow them to experience a close personal relationship with Him through Christ. As the end times approach, the Lord is going to do everything He is allowed by man to draw people nigh unto Him that they may have eternal life with Him. There will be those that we encounter that feel they have everything figured out and can determine whether God is doing something through you or whether God likes what God is doing through you. The Lord tells us to flee from people like these.

There is nothing more vicious that a Christian that has never grown and become a carnal Christian or believes they have come to a point where they are comfortable in church but have never accepted the work on the cross that Jesus did for us all. Many of these people have been saved, sanctified and become petrified over the years.

The leadership in many churches has already begun to walk in darkness failing to believe that Jesus and God will do the things He promises through His Holy Spirit. They are at a point that when things begin to change and bring about conviction from the Holy Spirit, the evil spirits in them begin to rise up and the retaliation begins. They then begin to justify that God needs their help in fixing their problems.

Many of these people have become so comfortable sitting in their pews that when the Lord begins to speak to them they simply cannot hear Him. The Lord says that people will suffer from a dullness of hearing. When they begin to shut out the things the Lord is trying to say, they are turned over to a reprobate mind.

Because they cannot hear the word of God and are not going to listen to Him, and probably haven't for a long time, the process of "Preacher Killing" begins! The actions they will take against you, as a minister, are explained in the scripture above. Jesus is real plain when He says that they know not the Father nor Him. They are lost people sitting in the pews, engaged in the leadership of the church who are in firm belief they are doing God a favor by getting the minister God sent out of the church. These people will not rely on God to get rid of somebody. They work with the opinion that God wants them to do the work. They usurp the authority of removing someone from the congregation or the ministry from God and take it upon themselves.

God's word says that when they take actions against someone, God will remove His anger from that person and place the person being hurt in a safe place. This shows that their efforts will be all in vain!

We are writing this book in an effort to expose the devil and his tactics in the church through God's people and those that claim to be God's people but really need a good spiritual check-up or overhaul.

Since most of this starts while Pastors are away for a while to conferences or vacation there are many Pastors that are surprised by the things that happened while they were away. So, let us begin our journey to see how the Devil will work!

One - Falling into Witchcraft

Galatians 3:1-3, *"Oh, foolish Galatians! What magician has cast a spell on you? For you used to see the meaning of Jesus Christ's death as clearly as though I had shown you a signboard with a picture of Christ hanging on the cross. Let me ask you this one question: Did you receive the Holy Spirit by keeping the law? Of course not, for the Holy Spirit came upon you only after you believed the message you heard about Christ. Have you lost your senses? After starting your Christian lives in the Spirit, why are you now trying to become perfect through your own human effort?"*

The Lord is coming down pretty hard on the people of the church in Galatia by wanting to know who has led them astray through deceitful tactics and manipulation. Once we are truly born again, we receive the Spirit of God, which will give us the discernment to tell the difference from that which is good and that which is evil. We are able to hear the voice of God and weigh the things out, by the scriptures that will allow us to know what is of God and what is not. Obviously the church in Galatia had turned to doing things the way man had figured they needed to be done. The issue here is of circumcision which the Jews had convinced them was essential for salvation.

We have become legalistic in our churches and in so doing have moved the ministerial positions to that of a messenger from God with deputized authority to that of a hireling that we pay to preach to us the things that are comfortable for us and nothing else. This is in spite of what they claim about it is ok to step on my toes and if you don't you are not doing your job. A word of caution is, those folks that make that proclamation will generally be yelling the loudest the first time you are standing on their toes. Of course, we all know it is not the toes we are aiming for but the heart of the person so the Holy Spirit will bring about conviction and repentance.

Instead of having churches set up the way God would have them to be, we are having the age long problems of a laymen wanting to control funding and assets from and within the church. This is not a new thing. It has been going on since the 3rd century AD where Deacons began to flex their muscles of

2

authority over the God given authority to the ministers He calls. The proclamation of the Deacons in position of authority allows for a "Deacon Possessed" Church and some real problems. This is one of the most important reasons we should be careful when selecting Deacons and other leaders within a church.

We were in one church that the chairman of deacons ran every deacon out of the church and still claimed to be chairman of deacons and have authority over the Pastor. My oh my! We have some misguided people within the churches that have been destroying God's messengers for a long time. They always vow to get even. If the Pastor or minister does not fit the mold they want, the destruction and murder begins. Jesus calls the people that do these things murderers.

One church we interviewed at threw a book on church doctrine to me and asked me about the doctrinal stance I took. I told them that they could place that book comfortably on the shelf that the doctrine I follow is taught in the Word of God and it alone. We were called to the church. People are searching for freedom but they want it without change. We have got to be loyal to God and lay the rudiments of the world aside to preach Christ and Him crucified. Forget the painful legalism, it causes big riffs.

Galatians 5:17, *"The old sinful nature loves to do evil, which is opposite from what the Holy Spirit wants. And the Spirit gives us desires that are opposite from what the sinful man desires. These two forces are constantly fighting each other, and your choices are never free from this conflict."*

Here is another reason that so many Pastors come under such vicious attacks. I don't believe that you can get any plainer than this. The old sinful nature loves to do evil. It is rebellion to those things that are of God. This is where we begin to see the line being drawn in church conflict. People begin to display their real fruit and Paul writes that the fruit of the flesh is obvious. If you look at the people that come against a minister and see how it affects them you can see the uneasiness of the spiritual warfare inside of them. Most often times they are really uptight, angry and even very confrontational about anything that is going on. This attitude is noticeable right off. Watch the people in the leadership and be alert to their actions. It is the little things that will tip you off. When you see them, start praying for them. When you have opportunity, find a way to be their friend, if they will let you. Many times, these people are really hard to get close to.

A good friend of ours used to say he was "To Blessed to Be Stressed!" I still love that saying. When we are blessed for what we are doing, we can be assured that we are walking with God. All good things come from God and will stand for eternity. When you

4

see a person that is walking around in peace, you know where they stand with the Lord and their relationship.

It is not up to us to say whether someone is saved or unsaved because that is between them and God. Watch their fruit and you can tell how they stand. Jesus said that you would know them by their fruit. The best way to deal with people like this, after they start their rebellion is to pray for them and be cautious in your dealings with them.

Galatians 5:19-21, *"When you follow the desires of your sinful nature, your lives will produce these evil results: sexual immorality, impure thoughts, eagerness for lustful pleasure, Idolatry, participation in demonic activities, hostility, quarreling, jealousy, outbursts of anger, selfish ambition, divisions, the feeling that everyone is wrong except those in your own little group, envy, drunkenness, wild parties, and other kinds of sin. Let me tell you again, as I have before, that anyone living that sort of life will not inherit the Kingdom of God."*

As people follow their desires to do things contrary to what God would have them to do, they begin to destroy themselves from within. More oftentimes than not, a church that will go through a crisis will continue in a crisis situation until they truly let God have the work back and follow Him and Him alone.

Evil results will manifest throughout the work as people begin to show up in rebellion against God's sent person. Many churches have forgotten that God sends preachers in to deliver messages and get a church to go where He would have it to go. I am not going to argue about the Christian Church verses the church of Satan. That is a non-issue to me. God has many churches that are riding in an area of "lukewarmness" right now and He is working to get them to move. He said in Zechariah 11 for the shepherd to take on the part of the worthless shepherd. We must know that God has the person selected for a church and that person, should they be of God and called of God will do the work for God that God wants done. Many times, after the aftermath, you may be left wondering!

I have seen many things that have caused divisions in churches. All of this can be attributed to the fruit that Paul writes about in the referenced scripture. These things will manifest themselves as soon as God is brought into a church that has been cold for many years.

The hostility and anger, the violent outbursts that take place within churches and more particularly within the sanctuaries of the churches are a great area of grief for me. People turn these places that are sanctuaries and turn them into houses and dens of iniquity as they push their own agendas. They are rough on anybody that is in the way. The Pastor becomes the target of their anger. There is provocation to get the Pastor to fall into traps they have laid for them. There has already been much backbiting and manipulation that has gone on before that. There have been many acts of demonic witchcraft done within the church itself and around the area. How bad do you think this grieves God?

People on their own agenda will begin to force people to take sides or put them on a side against them with their stand to ruin the Pastor's ministry and his/her reputation. There were people at a meeting one night praying for a Pastor as the Pastor was meeting in the fellowship hall located in another building. After the meeting there ended, the Pastor went back to the sanctuary and the people from the other building went in behind him. They were mad and they made sure they created a disturbance that night. The disturbance was so bad the ruckus went into the parking lot. The Pastor was referred to as Satan incarnate by a disgruntled member of the small group as they screamed at him in the parking lot. The aggravated group was grasping at all straws to get rid of this particular pastor but couldn't produce anything. I'm going to tell you that after 12 years in the Army and having seen many bad situations, I have seen better conduct coming from a group of sailors in a barroom brawl in some foreign country on payday night. It was the poorest display of Christian behavior I have ever seen in my life. There was no doubt the works of the flesh were manifest and obvious! By the time this situation had elevated to this level, the people had begun to attack those in the church that would not go along with them. Everybody becomes a target to these people. They are like spoiled children throwing a temper tantrum!

Everybody was wrong except this small group of people in their minds. This scripture doesn't hit on every bit of sin that takes place during these times of rebellion. Paul writes for the Lord about many in letters to other churches. The sin of Gossip becomes the worst sin of all as the bearing of false witness manifests against the minister. It is such a shame the way the devil gets into these situations and the lives of people calling themselves Christians or as the Word of God says, "Brothers and Sisters." When a situation gets like this, I try to do as Paul wrote for God in the Book of Corinthians to know not to eat with these people who call themselves brothers and sisters and continue on in sin. I begin to separate myself from them.

It is not my word, nor my judgment; it is the Word of God that says these people who do these things will not inherit the Kingdom of God. Keep your relationship in tact while these things go on around you. It will be tough and you will be pressured but there will be those that will rally with you and support you through these times. Keep your eyes on Jesus, your Savior and Deliverer.

Two - False Teachers in the congregation

Jude 8, 10, 12,18,19: *"Yet these false teachers who claim authority from their dreams, live immoral lives, defy authority, and scoff at the power of the glorious ones. But these people mock and curse the things they do not understand. Like animals, they do whatever their instincts tell them, and they bring about their own destruction. When these people join you in fellowship meals celebrating the love of the Lord, they are like dangerous reefs that can shipwreck you. They are shameless in the way they care only about themselves. They are like clouds blowing over dry land without giving rain, promising much but producing nothing. They are like trees without fruit at harvesttime. They are not only dead but doubly dead. For they have been pulled out by the roots. That in the last times there would be scoffers whose purpose in life is to enjoy themselves in every evil way imaginable. Now they are here, and they are the ones who are creating divisions among you. They live by natural instinct because they do not have God's Spirit living in them."*

The most misunderstood thing we address in the church today is false teaching. False Teachers are not only those that have positions in the pulpit ministry but many of them are your residential Theologians that feel they have God all figured out and are teaching wrong theology. They are teaching that there is a level of grace that doesn't exist in the church today. They teach that there is no need for teachers because we have the Holy Spirit to teach us, and radical things such as this. Yes, we do have the Holy Spirit to teach us! There is no doubt about that. He teaches us through conviction of the heart. He reveals things to us through revelational knowledge and through other people. These people are dangerous to the flock of Jesus as He is calling for them to come into the fold. These are the people that become legalistic and "handcuff" God in His work.

One of my favorite past times, as a Pastor was to go into the work place and observe the church leaders at work. You would be surprised what you will hear and see when you catch them a work. You would never know that some of them are even churchgoers yet alone bold enough in calling themselves Christian. These people feel they have the right relationship with God that allows them to live in a life of sin, rebelling against anything they do not like or understand and still be in fellowship with God. These always seem to be the very people that will question whether God can or would bring about an act of salvation in the life of someone they know well but claim to be righteous their self. They deny that Jesus could save that lost soul from the pits of hell. How insane! I believe that if someone is out of fellowship with God, it will be awfully hard for him/her to hear the last trumpet call from God when the church is called out. Where does this leave these types of people?

We were in a church once where we had prayed for a man for healing. The man was having bad chest pains and could hardly breath. He was in some real trouble. The Lord sent Cheryl and I by to pray for him and ask God for healing on his frail body. God immediately eased the pain and allowed the man to breath easily once again. The next day the man was getting around well. His wife gave a testimony to how God had worked in healing her husband and what had happened. Her brother, who was a deacon in the church, shouted out, we'll see if he's still alive when he supposed to go to the doctor next week. The unbelief of the Bible and what God is telling us is what is making false teachers. It is the fact that people want to say that God doesn't do those things any more. The other side of that is that God's grace is so sufficient that I can sin like the devil and still make it to heaven. These are both devil's lies! God is the same as He was when He made this place and He will remain the same. It is us that have changed our theology about Him. By the way, the man had been diagnosed with chronic lung problems, kidney problems and heart problems. The Lord chose to heal his kidney problem and his chronic lung problem. He did undergo by-pass surgery and received 5 bypasses. Today he is doing well at age 74. Praise Be to God!

Beware of these people that teach a different God from the one in the Bible. Beware if they tell you God has changed! They cannot support that at all! They might try to justify it in their finite minds but it simply cannot be done. Even the denominations that claim the Bible is the Infallible and Inerrant Word of God and it can only be read and interpreted literally cannot fully justify their theology using their standpoint. They may prove their doctrine that way but surely they cannot prove God that way. God is indeed the same. Surely the destruction of these people will be swift and accurate as the Lord does His work. You hear reported cases of sudden deaths from different churches as Pastors are driven out of the ministry. There seems to be an unexplainable amount of sickness and other affliction that seems to follow after church conflict. It is sad to see these things and hear them. God says that it is a terrible thing to fall in to the hands of a Living God!

One of the things people love to do is gather

for potluck dinners and the sort. These things are good but they are also open invitations to discuss theology and spark different debates along the way. In a lot of cases the Pastor has not been there long enough to establish a strong bond with the people and the church boss or false teacher must find out what the Pastor knows. It is during these times they will talk casually to you about the Lord all the while collecting ammunition against you to use later when they decide the time is right to get the Pastor out of the way. This will come as the Pastor is beginning to make some real headway in the church and God has been working. The Church boss, "False Teacher" will begin to become like a dog and become territorial and start marking his or her territory. All the while their plot to make sure you do not take their place as the leader of the congregation does not get thwarted. They have been through this before. They are well trained at what they are doing. They are going to get the Pastor no matter what it takes. They are going to drive the minister out of the ministry because they will not curtail the teachings they are pushing in the church. Yes, plain and simple, it is good versus evil. These people are after one thing and one thing only, self-gratification. The word of God says that Pride cometh before the fall. I believe that, don't you? These people will knock holes in the bottom of your ministry the Lord has placed you in and cause you to sink. They simply do not care. They are self-willed and self-centered. Sad enough, they do it with the blessings from many denominations today, in the name of money. These people, when compiled together will ultimately shipwreck an entire denomination.

In regards to celebrating Holy Communion with these people, In serving communion during a church crisis, God, through His Holy Spirit will bring about the desired results on His plan for the local assembly. Do not withhold the celebration and remembrance in fear of profaning the Body of Christ and deny the celebration of what Christ did for us. The Lord says that we should examine ourselves before taking part in communion and if we take it unworthily we would bring damnation unto ourselves. Our hearts should be clear of issues that separate us from Him prior to taking communion. He also goes on to say that this is why there are many among you that are sick and asleep (or dead). Be careful how you handle the sacraments. God will purge His Body of impurities.

Watch these people and what they do. They are the ones crying and screaming for the church to grow but yet they haven't brought anybody in for a long time, if ever. They have no way of producing anything because they cannot even water a seed to help it to grow.

We have been in churches where the people have promised all kinds of things to us. These false teachers, because of their status, have stopped things from happening through their tactics. They are the ones that are making the promises hollow for the church. These things damage the integrity of the church in its dealings. Again, we are back to a tree at harvest time. The Lord says they are a tree that has received everything it needed and still it did not produce fruit when it was supposed to. It is sad to say that many of these people are looked up to and when the need arises to help someone understand the work on the cross Jesus did for us, they cannot be effective in helping them to understand and Trust Jesus as their Savior and Lord. The Lord says they are not only dead to His work; they are dead in the spirit as well. They are doubly dead. They are no longer rooted in the Word of God nor do they have a firm relationship with God to move forward in their life. These people need to be replanted in good soil before it is too late.

Noah built the Ark and he preached for 120 years during that time. He didn't have but 8 people on that boat. Noah did not shut the door on the Ark, God did. God's door to grace slammed shut and the storm began. There will be a time, in everybody's life that the door of Grace will slam shut and you will either be inside or outside of God's saving grace. It appears that these false teachers are living in a world of falsehood from believing their own teachings. The only god they serve is the god called self.

People in the church are riding on a wave of

Grace that doesn't exist. There have come along people teaching that God's forgiveness is final. I believe that too! I believe that we are forgiven. The problem I have with this is we must first repent. We must honestly and sincerely turn away from what we were doing and start afresh our life. This is not what many people are teaching today.

It is funny to see the expression on a person's face when you go to them with a word from God and tell them about a situation that only they and God know about. The sad thing is the devil, through somebody, will steal that away from him or her and the minister appears to be the false teacher.

People today feel that God doesn't talk to people about them and they simply cannot know what is going on with them. God will do what it takes to draw His people to Him or make a decision one way or another anyway. They do things behind closed doors because nobody can see them, even God, they think.

These false teachers cause more church squabbles than enough. They will do anything it takes to get things together and get rid of the real person of God that is teaching the real truth as inspired by God. They do not care the damage it takes on the church and how it hurts the people. They are the ones that will allow Satan to work through them. Jude wrote for God saying that "Now" they are here and causing divisions among you. Now! They are hard at work taking hold of God's churches and destroying God's people and mostly they are destroying God's called people that serve the ministry.

These people are spiritually blind. They cannot see the Holy Spirit working anywhere. Hebrews says that without "Holiness" no man shall see the Lord. Unless we walk in that righteousness, we cannot see God working in and around us. We cannot even feel Him working in our lives. We would be spiritually dead and this is where the false teachers are now! They can only do things in the natural because they do not know the spiritual at all. They cannot think beyond self and getting things done in a worldly fashion. The sad thing to me is, most of these false teachers are lined up in the church leadership. God's word says that His Spirit is not in them!

You will be accused of being a false teacher many times in an adverse situation. It comes with the territory. Just remember that God called you and you were chosen to walk through the fire with Him during a tough time. Count it all joy!

Three - Luring You to Agreement

Matthew 18:19 *"I also tell you this: If two of you agree down here on earth connecting anything you ask my Father in heaven will do it for you."*

People will begin to ask you to pray for an unspoken request that is known to everybody in the click and the Pastor is not in the click so you are agreeing to a plot being offered up to God.

Looking back into the Book of Leviticus we will find the Aaron's two sons were in the tabernacle offering up strange incense to God when God came down as fire and devoured them. God's word also says that prayers are as incense sent up to the Lord. There is a real problem with us praying for something that we do not know what we are praying for. True, there are people that do not want their personal life revealed to the world and would like some things to be kept in a low key however, the notion that we can stand and offer prayers to the Lord and not know what they are is not a very wise move. As a Pastor, our instinct will tell us to be kind and compassionate and pray for the person's request but, how can you know what you are praying for? If you stand in agreement in prayer, asking God to move the Pastor out of the place in which God sent Him, you are now linked to this strange incense or profane prayer going up to God. Chances are, should you be lured into this situation, you will be burned in the fire. We can make many excuses for going ahead and answering these requests and we can justify in our hearts what God will do but we must justify it by His word and His word alone. I simply will not pray for unspoken requests when they are ask for and will ask the person that made the request about the prayer request after the service or meeting and then pray with them Be discerning about what you are praying for!

There will be someone that will ask to have prayer for the church, which is lightly and loosely interpreted to mean that person is probably disgruntled with things and is beginning to grumble for their own benefit behind the scene.

This is generally one of the first signs that someone is stirring up trouble in the church. Some person will stand and request prayer for this "little church." They are really alerting the people that there is a declaration of war going on right then and there. There has been a rebellion brewing and the armies of attack are being launched to begin their mission. It seems that the person that makes this announcement is generally a gullible spokesperson for a person that is working behind the scenes without the courage to stand and speak for their self. This person becomes the messenger for the devil in his attack against God's work. These signs will generally begin as the church is in a growth pattern and is turning some corners it hasn't even seen for a long time.

We know of one church that grew from 54 in worship on Sunday to 123 in worship on Sunday in 3 and half months. There was prayer being answered instantaneously and healings were taking place all around. People began to call the people in the church because they had become known as the church that got answers to their prayers. There was a literal revival going on and then, some henchman in the church began to be a patsy spokesman and deliver such messages as the one above. It was in no time the revival was stopped and the church began to dwindle. The Pastor and his family were run off and another Pastor came. They struggled calling their selves doing well and they finally split. They had the same problem with a different Pastor and the ultimate split came anyway. God will have His way, whether you are the chosen one to carry out His plan or they delay it for a small season, He will prevail! He promises that He is the victor!

There will be those that will become focused on the finances of the church requesting prayer in that area. This generally interprets to Pastor, I have quit giving a tithe and you better hope someone comes along to make up the difference. I love this prayer request. It generally comes when someone wants to become boastful about how much money they are giving to the church. How they are tithing and how their tithe will be missed if things don't change and change in a hurry. If I were that disgruntled at a church and Pastor, I would go and find another place and leave the Pastor alone as opposed to stealing money from God. The first revelation of a spiritual problem to the public is to stand in church and say that we need to pray for the finances of the church. This is the surest sign that people do not believe that God will provide for His work on earth. They simply believe that the money they have belongs to them and not God. These people are not tithers, they are not even givers, they are people who try to manipulate God with their money giving. They are much like the Pharisee beating himself on the chest and telling God how lucky He is to know him.

A Big newsflash! Never have I prayed for the finances of a church! I believe God will provide for everything that He wants the church to do. God may not give money because He wants us to stay in a state of worship for a while and draw close to Him before we go out. Jesus said in Acts 1:8 that when the Holy Spirit comes upon you, then you can be witnesses. There are many churches that are powerless and need to get back to the word of God and regain His power to be able to witness, even in their own communities. The Power of the Lord is missing from the churches today. Money does not get power from God, only worldly things. Money cannot help us be a witness until we become empowered and then it can only be used as a tool. People are wrapped up in the world today and money. It is a terrible thing to say that we have regressed as churches to being overly concerned over someone's tithe coming in.

If there is someone in your church that wants to quit tithing, let him or her do so. It does no good to lecture or preach on tithing. Once God gets a hold on their life, He will get their pocketbook, without restriction and reservation. The finances of the church are God's problem; He knows what is going on. It is our position to be good stewards of what God has allowed us to have.

There could be a good reason to look at the finances and determine whether you and your church are in line, if possible. There are many churches that feel the Pastor has no right to even see the mail let alone the bank statement when it comes in. As the

Pastor, you are entitled to all things that go on in the church so you, as a Pastor will know how to pray. You are the under shepherd of the flock and you cannot adequately take care of the flock not having your God given Pastoral Authority.

Four - Enduring Persecution

Matthew 5:10-12; *"God blesses those who are persecuted because they live for God, for the Kingdom of Heaven is theirs. God blesses you when you are mocked and persecuted and lied about because you are my followers. Be happy about it! Be very glad! For a great reward awaits you in heaven, And remember, the ancient prophets were persecuted, too."*

Just Yesterday we had another American man beheaded in a foreign country. This would be the kind of persecution that we would think Jesus was talking about in the Beatitudes. We know that with the exception of one of Jesus' Disciples they all suffered martyrs' deaths by being beheaded and even hung on a cross like him as legend and history reports Peter was done, except he was allegedly hung upside down. Some of them were stoned and the sword killed some.

The one that was not killed this way was sent into exile on the Island of Patmos where he wrote about the Revelation. This Disciple was referred to as the Disciple Jesus loved and we know him as St John or John the Revelator. The pattern seems clear that we will all endure some form of persecution while following Christ, some more severe than others.

We have a Pastor friend that was Pastoring in a mid-western state that upon his arrival there were 8 people attending the church. Some of those people were upset with him shortly after he arrived over his preaching. They got together and went down and took out a full page add in the newspaper for a Sunday. The add named his church and advised people not to go there because the "Anti-Christ" was preaching there. He endured that persecution and had a great ministry there that led to even a greater ministry in a new location.

On a district we once served, there was a Pastor that had a son of a board member that got mad at him and the son went to see the Pastor. The Pastor, unsuspectingly opened the door to his parsonage, his four children and wife standing close by only to be gunned down by this disgruntled son. This man suffered the persecution that we would call extreme. His family will remember that day the rest of their lives as well.

In the same timing, a Pastor's son was stabbed in the head with a screwdriver at school and was left in the hallway with no assistance until another parent saw the young boy lying in the hall. The boy died due to the lack of action by people.

Now that you have heard these tidbit stories, I want to touch on some areas that perhaps you are familiar with.

I got to the point where I would not let anyone do the church bulletin for me except my wife. It is the only way that you can really ensure that unhealthy things are not going out through the bulletins. If a crisis begins to develop in your church, the person making the bulletin is subject to start placing things in it that are not pre-approved and support the agenda of the faction and division that is in place. Safe guard your bulletin or hire a church secretary that you can tell what to put into the bulletin. To often the person with the bulletin turns it into a message center instead of a worship tool.

What kind of stuff do you see in these bulletins you might ask? Well, there are many scriptures that you can place that will cause people to know what is going on without being really obvious. Of course, the first thing they will try to do is call you the devil himself. They will generally go to such scriptures as the messengers of Satan come disguised as angels of light. They might make more blatant comments but not generally. They want to leave room for wiggling out of the situation or having a good comeback. At the first sign of this, you should begin praying and perhaps even start doing the bulletin yourself.

I have seen the people that prepare these bulletins use them to make announcements against the Pastor and call meetings without the Pastor's foreknowledge. All this is very devious and very damaging. I can only say that God admonishes us to know those that labor among us.

Another area that will become obvious for you will be the private meetings that people will begin to have. They think you are blind and do not see what they are doing. If you are trying to do your job as a Pastor, you may very well walk into one of these meetings and accidentally break it up for a while. These meetings are common in smaller churches where they can gather around a table after church and start taking care of the church business. This will be a beginning phase of what we covered in previous chapters.

These private meetings are not the will of God. He is not happy with them as they take place. There is stuff leading up to the control and manipulation of the Pastor and the ministry because they own the church building and the Pastor is a guest there. He has got to do things to please the people and not God. They really are not too concerned about God's want at this time, just their own. You cannot stop these meetings from taking place. God is the only one that will stop them and we are never sure about His timing on these issues. Don't get caught up on what they are doing. Know in your heart that God sent you there and that God will keep you there. God will protect you from them.

Grow close to the Father during these times and let them alone.

They will eventually begin to shun you and your family giving you the cold shoulder treatment. Find some friends outside of the church and leave the church behind. Don't worry about what your congregation is going to say, you are serving them and are entitled to time off and a family life. Take your day off and stick to it. If something comes up and you absolutely need to be there, make sure you get another day off and do it soon.

Cheryl and I went to a seminar taking vacation from Tuesday through Saturday. We had a regular day off that we never took on Monday. This particular week we left on Monday and the entire church got upset because we went on vacation a day early. When their mind is made up on what they want to do, God is no longer the director but the spectator because they will not consult Him and could not hear Him if they did.

Not to mention that as a Minister you are subject to be accused of everything in the world. My goodness the things that people have accused me of doing. Had I done a small portion of what has been said about me, I would be in a jail somewhere doing some real hard time. I want you to know, there is no end to the length that a backslidden Christian will go to destroy a ministry. It is always followed by the comment that you will never Pastor another church again. This reveals the real character and position they perceive their selves as having. They have just become, in their mind, the person that calls people into the ministry and sends them out. They are the ones that now own every church. How reprobate can you truly become?

Then when all of this is going on, you must find a place where you can draw a line in the sand. How far does persecution go and where does the law step in?

This is where denominational leadership gets a little upset with Pastors in handling things. Do you idly stand by and receive threats and harassing phone calls as people come against you and place your family in danger? I think NOT! If you are anything like me, I will do what I have to do to protect my family. I realize, that many times, that which is accessible to us at the time restricts us. Many times we cannot move and get on the road without money. People have told me to load up whatever I could in my car and get out of town. There is an issue of money to leave and an issue of money once we get to where we are going. There are moral obligations from the church and there are many other reasons that we can relate to. I just want to say, if man tells you to go and you go, shame on you! If God tells you to leave all your stuff and go, then get moving.

There is a chapter in the Bible that bridges the church to the secular law. That Book and Chapter is Romans 13. It is the one that tells us to obey the authorities. In fact, God refers to these authorities as ministers. You have the right to protection for you and your family. It is not against the law for you to take action. It will be hard and you will run into many obstacles. But, there is recourse despite the reluctance of the officials! The denominational leadership will not help you in these situations for the most part, many times because they cannot and most times they really don't want to lose the financial support. They are able to help you from time to time through forced termination programs if they are available. This should always be a last resort and not used until told to by the Lord.

The Lord says to count all these things joy! If we keep the Lord in our focus as we walk through the

fires of persecution, we will come out on the other side
unharmed.

Five - The Test of Faith

Job 1:1-12, 22: *"Satan replied to the Lord, 'Yes, Job fears God, but not without good reason! You have always protected him and his home and his property from harm. You have made him prosperous in everything he does. Look how rich he is! But take away everything he has, and he will surely curse you to your face!' "All right, you may test him,' the Lord said to Satan. 'Do what you want with everything he possesses, but don't harm him physically.' So Satan left the Lord's presence. In all of this, Job did not sin by blaming God."*

Poor Job! He had everything that was going his way. The old devil himself shows up and wants to talk to God about the situation. He informs God about how good He has always been to Job and how Job really loves the Lord. The devil is of the opinion that if Job should loose everything he had, he would not love God so much. He even felt that perhaps Job would even come to a point that he would curse God and turn away from God.

What appeals to me about this account of persecution is, Job was pitted between the devil and God to satisfy the lusts of the devil against Job. He was sure that once God began to take away the earthly possessions that Job had that he would have a change of heart. Praise the Lord the devil cannot read our heart! How can a man lose everything and still love God? That is what the devil is trying to show cannot be done. He was convinced that he could get Job away from God. It was not so much the faith of Job to God that reached out and grabbed me so much as the faith that God had in Job. I believe He says, have you considered my servant Job?

In one day, Job lost his home, his wife and his family. He lost everything that he owned. How would you like to have a day like that? Perhaps you have! Perhaps you have returned back to you church provided home to find all your stuff on the front lawn and maybe even rained on and not much good anymore. The situation could be added to, I'm sure. Maybe you know of someone else that has had these struggles in the service of God. Maybe you have heard the voice of God saying, have you considered my servant Job? God had more faith in Job that it wasn't the things of the world he loved but the God of the Universe. God knew, without hesitation that Job was the man for the job. When God sends you to a place to do His work, He has hand-picked you and knows that you are the one that will accomplish that which He has assigned you. If things look to sour on you and you have been following God's leading, know that God choose you to do some tough work for Him. Not everybody gets the glamorous jobs for God; somebody has got to do the hard and thankless work for Him. He may have chosen you! He has great faith in us! Stand firm and stay committed to your calling. Renew it daily with the Lord. It would please the devil to see you throw in the towel and say you are done. It would break God's heart. ☹

The Lord believed so much in Job that God allowed Job to go through some very trying times. The devil could take anything except the health and life of Job. This kind of thing did not happen to people unless they were deeply rooted in sin so this also brought criticism from the outside people looking at him. He was pressured from all sides. He was compressed but never crumbled! Oh, that man Job and what he endured, all because the devil would have sworn that Job would curse God.

There is nothing more agonizing as a Pastor than to have to leave a church after it was doing so well and someone decided to be used by the devil and stop what was going on. Most Pastors, including us, sold our home and everything else we owned except a few meager possessions to go into the ministry. The first church we were at, the people decided it was time for us to leave and they would not give a reason or tell us what we had supposedly done. I may address this more later but our daughter Jessica talks about it in her book, "Living Behind the Glass Walls." Anyway, I heard all about how I done so much and how I should have done things and how I could have been wrong. Much of what was given, as advice was what we had been doing but still we were under some tough persecution. The persecution was to the point that I told our District Superintendent that we were only 9 funerals away from a complete revival, talking about the board members. I did not gain much support that way for sure.

The long and short is, I hadn't done anything wrong to my knowledge, felt that I had followed what the Lord had told me and was still doing God's work. I was catching flack from everywhere and everyone. Nobody understood the dilemma except a Pastor 12 miles away. He prayed with me and spoke with me. He detailed the very moves of the people as they executed their plan. He was always telling me their very next move. These people tried to get the FBI after me and anybody else they could find trying to look into my past. They were not successful. That was the first time someone threatened me with the FBI and was not successful. The second time, my brother was in the middle of a background investigation to work for the FBI and we were being investigated as well. They were not aware of that.

As we walk through trying times in the ministry, it is imperative that we look towards the final goal and that is seeing Jesus. We must hold in our heart the calling that God called us to through Christ and believe that we are just going on to something better. Job did not sin by blaming God for the situation. It is easy to talk to God and seek His wisdom on a situation but it may be years before He gives you a full picture of things.

It had been four years since we had problems in our first church. From time to time the Lord would ask me if I loved the people at that church. I would tell Him yes. He would ask me if I thought I would be able to Pastor them again. I would always tell Him no. One day He asked me again and I said yes. He told me then that I was now healed from that wound and that we needed to move on with the ministry. Praise the Lord!

Six - Who is this Guy Who's Talking to the Lord?

IS 14:12-14 & 22 *"How you are fallen from heaven, O shinning star, son of the morning! You have been thrown down to the earth, you who destroyed the nations of the world. For you said to yourself, 'I will ascend to heaven and set my throne above God's stars. I will preside on the mountain of the gods far away in the north. I will climb to the highest heavens and be like the Most High.' This is what the Lord Almighty says: 'I myself, have risen against him! I will destroy his children and his children's children, so they will never sit on his throne."*

This guy Satan! How did he get an audience with God anyway? Where did he come from and what does he do?

We find the Lord speaking to us in Isaiah 14 about who the devil is and how he got to the earth. Satan was an angel in heaven that was close to God. He was the one that led praises for God. As you see, he said that he would climb up and place his throne above God's throne and be like God Himself. Satan was an angel in rebellion against God and His established authority. Satan was once one of the Arch Angels in heaven. There were three of them that we know about in the Bible. There was Michael, the Warrior, Gabriel, the Messenger and Lucifer the Praise Leader. This may be starting to raise some curiosity as you read on. We know that Michael will be here forever along with Gabriel. Lucifer was cast down because of rebellion. Sin had not been established but this is the very essence of sin, rebellion. All sin starts as an act of rebellion to God's authority. Nothing more or nothing less than rebellion! This is what makes sin across the board equal in God's site as it all comes from rebellion.

As Lucifer came up and decided to move up on his own will and own way to the top, disregarding any instruction from God and forgetting whom the Creator is caused God to rise up against him. God said He would destroy any of his successors so that there would be no other after him. God will destroy the devil in his entirety one day and there will never be another. There was no longer a place for Lucifer in heaven and will never be and one day there will be no place for him on earth. He took approximately one third of the angels with him as he fell. He is quite a deceiver.

A story goes: a little lady that never said anything bad about anybody went on to church one Sunday morning. As she arrived two of the Ushers were speaking about her never being negative and always finding something nice to say about people. They decided to ask her if she could say anything nice about the devil. Without a moments' hesitation she answered Yep! He's a hard worker!

We see the manifestation of Lucifer through our churches many times through the music leader of the church. There are many music leaders and ministers of music that think that they are higher than the Pastor in the chain of authority. They go in and usurp the authority of God and have caused many Pastors to fall. The day will come when the Almighty God will throw those people down and ensure that no others of them will come into that position. No doubt, I am going to make a minister of music mad here and that is all right. They are useful and can enhance the work of the Lord when they work as a team.

I remember going into a church where the music minister asked me how I felt sharing the pulpit with her. I told her I felt it was the other way around and that I had no problem as long as she worked in cooperation with me. She got off on her own agenda and had done some things one night in the church that brought her down by defying the authority of God through the scriptures given to Pastors. There is more to falling in these positions than getting put out of the job.

Now don't get me wrong when I speak about these music ministers, there are more good ones than bad ones! There are many great people of God doing God's work every chance they get! But this is where I see an area of concern within church authority. There is too much liberty from and with the pulpit. I have adopted the idea and procedure of placing the music leader away from the pulpit and in plain view of the congregation. This removes the thought of the "power of the pulpit" so to speak.

This guy is the deceiver, the anti-Christ, the son of perdition, the lawless one, the bloody man, the wicked one, the man of the earth, the enemy, the adversary, the violent man, the Assyrian, the king of Babylon, son of the morning, the spoiler, the little horn, the vile person, the willful king, the idle shepherd, the angel of the bottomless pit, and a various number of other things.

He speaks to God as the accuser of the brother and tries to remind God of how bad we are. Jesus is the mediator that keeps us clean through God's Grace and Faith along with repentance.

I can only imagine the devil and his attitude towards God and just barging into the room where He is and start talking regardless of what God is up to. It is almost like being on the telephone and having a television going full blast and having one of your children come and ask for permission to do something that you would normally say no to but you couldn't hear and said yes. It is aggravating and that is what I see the devil doing here with God.

This is the serpent in the Garden of Eden that caused the fall of man by deceiving Eve and getting her to eat of the forbidden fruit by telling a half-truth. Satan still works the same way today through people. Whatever you do, please remember that Satan uses people just as the Lord does and he will be more than happy to let them take a personal attack for it. They are not the bad ones, it is the devil through them that is acting up and they are not aware entirely of what is going on.

Seven - Walking through the Fire

Dan. 3:1-6; *King Nebuchadnezzar made a gold statue ninety feet tall and nine feet wide and set it up on the plain of Dura in the province of Babylon. Then he sent messages to the princes, prefects, governors, advisors, counselors, judges, magistrates, and all the provincial officials to come to the dedication of the statue he had set up. When all these officials had arrived and were standing before the image King Nebuchadnezzar had set up, a herald shouted out, "People of all races and nations and languages listen to the king's command! When you hear the sound of the horn, flute, zither ,lyre, harp, pipes, and other instruments, bow to the ground and worship King Nebuchadnezzar's gold statue. Anyone who refuse to obey will immediately be thrown into a blazing furnace."*

One of the first things that I noticed as I studied through the 3rd Chapter of Daniel was the group of people that the king had ordered to be at the ceremony revealing the statue he had made. Looking deep into this, we can see that the people present are all those that can effect the lives of the ones around them. We are seeing the politicians and the law enforcers at the ceremony. Of course the three Hebrews were there too! Daniel was off gallivanting across the countryside or something but wasn't present during this chapter at all. This is the only chapter in Daniel that Daniel was not around.

The decree went out from the king that when the music sounded that everybody would bow down to the statue. Now, this is important about the people. This is something that happens even today in our churches. It is called denominational doctrine and dogmatics. The top-level leadership will establish things and then dictate that these things must happen within the church or else. Many times the punishment can become severe or you may even be excused from your position. Anyway, you will go through the fire. We find three young men that were ready to stand firm, believing that the God of Abraham, Isaac and Jacob would deliver them that day. They didn't know how or any other details, just that He would deliver them.

Understanding that the Hebrews were now in captivity, these men were in high government positions. They were right there with the king and his men. As the Hebrews were brought out of Jerusalem and taken into captivity, they were screened and only the cream of the crop was brought into Babylon. They had freedom to own property, work jobs, have money and even have high power political positions but yet were in bondage. It sure sounds a whole lot like the modern times to me along with the captivity that the sin nature brings.

These three men, despite the decree from the king stood steadfast on the Word of God and would not budge as the music played. This enraged the Chaldeans that stood and watched as the ceremony was taking place. If you want to be noticed in a crowd, just don't do what the crowd does and listen to someone yell. These guys went straight to the top to get action taken and ensure the king carried out the decree he had made that anyone that would not bow down would be thrown into the fiery furnace.

The king spoke to these men as an effort to get them to bow down to the statue but they still refused. The king became angry and ordered the fire to be turned up seven times hotter than usual. This still did not intimidate the Hebrew men. They continued to believe God for deliverance. They were willing to take a stand for the Almighty God that could and would deliver them from all evil. These are the kind of leaders we need today within our churches. We need leaders that are bold enough to stand and say that right is right and wrong is wrong. We need the kind of leaders that are not afraid of the fire and will be willing to go through it should the need arise. Jesus tells us to pick up our cross and follow Him. I am firmly convinced that at some point, we will have to be willing to hang on that cross that God may be glorified through what He has done. No, we cannot save anyone and we will not be hung on a cross, at least I hope not but, in the spiritual realm, we must be ready, willing and able to go through these times to stand up for Him.

We must be willing to believe that God will provide all we need and that He will deliver us with His mighty right hand. Once we can grasp that, we too can be like the three Hebrews and speak with that same confidence and boldness standing for the Living God who will save us.

These poor guys were about to be thrown into a big furnace to be killed that had been turned up some seven times hotter than normal. Cremation temperature is around 1500 degrees and this furnace was estimated to be around 1800 degrees. It was more than hot enough to cook them to ashes. The king ordered that they be put into the furnace because they would not bend or bow to his man-made god. He was so angry that they were bound with all their clothes on. They still had hats and shoes. These guys had all the reason to burn fast. The guards opened the doors and the fire came up and killed them as the Hebrews fell into the furnace. The king's desire was to destroy them without a trace of them being left.

This is the way that church battles get. The people that are out to destroy you will pull out all the stops and turn up the heat as high as they can. They will get you so bound up that you cannot hardly preach and then attack you about your poor preaching. They will work hard to get you to be persuaded and turn to their way of thinking. This is exactly what the king was doing. Don't ever believe that church people will not turn up heat and even go so far as to threaten or kill a Pastor. We know of several cases that Pastors have been murdered literally and we can tell you of at least two death threats we have received from so called Christians. It all begins from false gods disguised in some form or fashion. Many times, and I would even go as far as to say most times, it is someone that everybody in the church is following that gets mad and you cannot do anything to them without some real harsh treatment. The faster and cleaner these people can get rid of you, the better. You must go before the truth is found. They are blind! The truth will be found out anyway! Be encouraged because God's plan will not be thwarted.

As the king looked into the furnace, he began to speak to his council. Remember, this was his decree, he ordered the men thrown into the furnace and now, he instantly wants to start dragging his council into the situation. He knows that he is in trouble. He asks how many men did WE throw into the furnace. You see, he knew there were only 3 but now he saw four. He even proclaimed that the forth one was an image like unto the Son of God. This man, who had never seen Jesus, because Jesus had yet come in the flesh recognized the Lord and Savior of this world. The king was astonished as he looked into the furnace. He not only saw 4 men, he saw them walking around unbound, no ties holding them, perhaps they were even singing praise songs, we don't know. We do know this; Jesus was with them in the toughest of times for them. It is important as we walk through tough times in the Pastoral ministry that people can see Jesus walking with us through these fires. It is easy to fall into the same traps and begin to act as a person in the flesh. It is a natural thing called survival that will get you, if you are not cautious.

There was a female minister that called me one time to ask about a bad situation she was in. She had sent out resumes across the United States looking to see where the Lord would lead her. She was telling me her options and that she really didn't want to go here or there. She wanted to go another place and she wanted to make sure that God was the one opening the door for her. I can go along with this to some point. She was in the fire too! She was looking for the door out. As the Hebrews walked around in that furnace, the king decided that his punishment could not override the grace of our God. He had the door open for the Hebrew men to come out, which they did. They came out of that furnace untouched, their clothes were fine and God says they didn't even smell like smoke. They got a promotion out of it as well and God was glorified. This doesn't mean that the king accepted God as the supreme being of his life, he had just made an acknowledgement. The real lesson here is, the same enemy that threw you into the furnace will have to let you out. The king spent some years out eating grass before he came to believe in God and was restored to his throne as king. The Hebrew men didn't say that they wanted to make sure that God was opening the door of the furnace to get out of that fire. They never hesitated as they were told to come out. Man opened that door for them. I am confident that God moved the hearts of those men but many times we see results that come through men and we tend to discount them and stay in that fire. I told that minister, when the door opens, get out and go!

This kind of commitment will help you to grow in your own faith and relationship with God through Christ. People will begin to see God through you and God will be glorified. This kind of peace in times of trials and the deliverance will help others to want what you have through those times their selves, when they come. This will draw people into a relationship that can only be achieved through Christ Jesus and His work on the Cross for us and His shed Blood.

Church leaders and church bosses along with denominational and convention leaders will place things on you from time to time that are not backed theologically and can prove to be more of a tradition of man than the Doctrine and Commandments of God. These things, if not adhered to will bring about persecution. It is up to you and me to stand firm on the Word of God and the Rock of our Salvation and let God do the rest of the work. The crux of the whole leadership thing is, if you can get the bosses to cower down, you now have the people. The three Hebrew men kept this from being a success in the king's situation. We are called to not bow or bend to man's rule or law in out Christian lives.

Eight - The Two Staffs

Zechariah 11: 7-14, *"So I cared for the flock intended for slaughter – the flock that was oppressed. Then I took two shepherd's staffs and named one Favor and the other Union. I got rid of their three evil shepherds in a single month. But I became impatient with these sheep-this nation-and they hated me too. So I told them, 'I won't be you shepherd any longer. If you die, you die. If you are killed, you are killed. And those that remain will devour each other!' Then I took my staff called Favor and snapped it in two, showing that I had revoked the covenant, I had made with all nations. Those who bought and sold sheep were watching me, and they knew that the Lord was speaking through my actions. And I said to them, 'If you like, give me my wages, whatever I am worth; but only if you want to.' So they counted out for my wages thirty pieces of silver. And the Lord said to me, 'Throw it to the potters – this magnificent sum at which they valued me!' So I took the thirty coins and threw them to the potters in the Temple of the Lord. Then I broke my other staff, Union, to show that the bond of unity between Judah and Israel was broken."*

Going into a new Pastorate you always go with a renewed spirit that has positive vibes about it and the motivation to do God's work has intensified. You have arrived at the new Pastorate with this intensified power. There is a degree of new freedom in which to operate. God is blessing. The church is beginning to grow and even a miracle or two might have happened. Your conversion rate is up and the baptistery stays full for the people needing to be baptized.

It won't take long to find out the plans the Lord has for this flock of people. He will work to help them get into a lifestyle and worship style that will bring glory to Him and bring about a much-needed change in many lives within the work. All you have to do is go and visit those that left the church and it won't take long to find out what is going on. These flocks that God has positioned all over this world are being prepared for slaughter. He is trying to break the spirit of oppression that they will be able to eat and be free. He has endowed the shepherd with two staffs. The first was Favor. God begins to give and show favor to these oppressed works that they might see and the yoke of bondage be broken away from them. He does mighty and powerful things in the midst of the people. He may even do a miracle in one of their lives.

We have seen people in these churches that have been healed both miraculously and instantaneously but because of the oppression will not stand up and give God the glory for it. These people will not even give testimony outside of the church for fear that others in the church may finally hear it and ridicule them. It is really sad that people will cower down instead of stand up!

God says that He will deliver or has delivered you from three evil shepherds in one month. God did and does today move in these great ways. Our problem is we have a bad habit of reaching up and grabbing someone the Lord has removed from the work and drag them right back, bringing compromise and giving him or her more control. If God takes them out, leave them alone. God says He has become impatient with these sheep. This takes me to Revelation and the church in Laodicea. Jesus said I would rather you be hot or cold, if your lukewarm, I will spew you out of my mouth. This is what is going on around the churches today. God is getting impatient with the people in the churches and wants them to move forward with Him. He wants them to be white-hot for God. But the sad thing about this is that God identifies that these sheep hated Him too! This means they are more than likely haters of men as well. At least that is what the Bible says will happen. God told them that He would not be their shepherd any longer.

This takes me to 1 Samuel and the account of Eli. When he received word the Ark of the Covenant had been captured, his daughter in law went into labor and died having her son but the son was named, Ichabad. The name means, the Glory of God has left this place. People do not want to hear this because they believe God will never leave them nor forsake them no matter how bad they act. This is the absolute truth. It is not He that moved however. The shepherd abandoned the flock to tend to itself. They are destined to self-destruct as they attack each other with no one to watch after them. There is simply no love and no guidance for direction. There is no protection afforded to this flock. Many churches are in this category today. They do have a way out through repentance but generally the arrogance in the work is so strong that only God can deal with them and He may choose not to at all, as He says.

God breaks the staff of favor and the door to grace will surely be slammed shut in the face of these people. This breaking of the staff of favor is the revocation of the covenant that God made with the people.

It is funny at times how when a church falls into a bad relationship with the Lord the first person they begin to get to is the Pastor. Here we see the shepherd being watched by people. They were fully aware that God was working through him. How many times have you went and spoken with someone or prayed with them and the Lord answered and did great and mighty things through you? People see these things and yet in still will stand up against the shepherd the Lord has sent. The first place they begin to manipulate a minister in is the area of finances. People in the flock will begin to withhold tithe money or place it into a different account to keep the minister from getting any money. They have broken a covenant with God to take care of the minister. It is not the minister that they are breaking that promise with, it is God Himself. God is speaking of the price that Jesus was sold out for by Judas but is also referring to the sum or petty sum that people sell pastors out for. They will not give freely any longer so the money they are now giving is really blood money and not honored by God. When people do tithe in these situations it is not with a cheerful heart but one with a strong amount of restraint.

This is where church splits begin to happen. As you notice, the church has already fallen out of favor from God, the covenant has been revoked and the iniquity in the house of God is deep. There are people that begin to fall in the conviction of the Holy Spirit and want to get back to a relationship and in fellowship with God. They begin to seek. The earnest talking takes place and then divisions start in the work. God says He will break or did break the staff of unity thereby causing a split in the nations or the church. The situation will escalate from this point. God is no longer in the picture or the church and all chaos will come about during this time of transition and may never be restored.

Nine - Exposing Devilish Behavior

Eph 4:17-19; *With the Lord's authority let me say this: Live no longer as the ungodly do, for they are hopelessly confused. Their closed minds are full of darkness; they are far away from the life of God because they have shut their minds and hardened their hearts against him. They don't care anymore about right and wrong, and they have given themselves over to immoral ways. Their lives are filled with all kinds of impurity and greed.*

As all of the things we have been talking about in this book begin to come to pass, there will be things that become clearly identifiable as changes from the norm. I will address some of these for you from A to Z. I will not elaborate to long on any of them but this is a pattern in which you will see the Devil work in church problems.

a. People who were initially having lunch with you will stop: When you first arrive in a church it seems that everybody wants to have lunch with the Preacher. Some of them will even buy your lunch for you. When they get to know you and decide that they are not in favor of something about you, and that can be anything, people will begin to drift from the after-church lunch time together.

b. These people will begin to grow in number as the church grows: As people begin to see a shift in the church begin to happen, they will start having their own lunch gatherings after church and talk about what they are going to do to keep control and possibly get rid of the Pastor.

c. The "Old Guard" will take their places: These people will mount up and start having recruiting meeting as they try to strengthen their guard status. They will use friendship first and foremost against the Pastor making comments like, I have known you for a long time and that guy just got here and whom are you going to believe, him or me.

d. They will stop wanting the minister to visit: The "old guard" will have the minister stop coming by or maybe not be home when they do come by. I have known of people to not answer their doors and refuse to answer their phones when the Pastor calls. They have already fired you at this point and it is their plan to get everyone to go along with them even if it has to destroy the church to carry it out.

d. They will begin having meetings and phone calls behind your back: You will drive around and see members cars at other people's houses or perhaps even a secluded place where the people think you would never find. They will be drafting up their war plan to bring a battle to you. They will be working hard to put you on the defense right off through a well-executed offense. A word to the wise, don't get caught up defending things they say about you, let them prove the validity of the accusation. Shakespeare once said, "I thinkest thou doest protest too much."

e. They will be making an all out effort to stop the forward movement of the church because they are loosing control of "their" church: Too often I have heard the comment that people want their church back, the Pastor is taking it away from them. How irrational can you get? The Pastor's name is not on anything. They own no building in most cases, and if they did, the congregation wouldn't be acting this way. It is a control issue that is driven by the change that God is bringing about. Back to the two staffs and people seeing God working through the minister. They just cannot see it for their own blindness.

f.   If they have received anything belonging to the pastor or his/her family, they will return it no longer desiring to have ties to them: Should anyone in the church have borrowed something from the Pastoral family or even given something, more than likely they will bring it back and return it to you. Even if you gave it to them as a gift, they will insist that they never took it that way and they have no need for it. They will be nice about it but what they are trying to do is cut ties with you.

h.   They will ask for prayer for the church and unspoken requests: Don't get caught up praying for something you know nothing about. Research the facts before you pray.

i.   The leadership has other things to do, which keeps them from praying with the pastor: The leadership will not want to pray anything in agreement with the Pastor for fear people might think they are siding with him or her. They do not want to even give prayer support to God's work, only their agendas.

j.   They will begin small investigations behind your back to question your credibility: I have had people threaten me with so many of the big initial guys like the IRS, FBI and others that I told them one day I must go and get a haircut because they would threaten to have the SPCA on me next if I didn't. None of these agencies will get involved in a church dispute. You will be lucky to get a police officer involved even in a threat towards you. The government honors separation of church and state until it gets physical. Unless you are wanted and wrongfully in the ministry, these threats are only harassment to you but there is not much you can do about them either.

k. They will begin to spread rumors that they grab on to: People will be messengers of the devil by taking a half-truth and running with it. We had one lady that called a friend of ours in Texas and asked him did he know us well and real well. When he answered yes, she said she didn't need to talk to him and hung up. She was only looking to find half-truths and people that didn't particularly care for us. A big news flash! I am like the Apostle Paul, I will either be used to start a riot or revival, there seems to be no middle ground with us.

l. They will begin to threaten and fail to support the ministry: As they see that some of these tactics are failing, the tithing will begin to fall. All this will come so fast it will be hard to identify which actually comes first. They will not do anything the Pastor would like to see done.

This is rebellion at its best.

m. They will begin to threaten you with the things in the past: As they feel they have information on you, even though it is not supported, they will begin to threaten you with your past.

n. They will start demanding you leave: As these attempts to put pressure on you fail they will begin to demand you leave. Many times they will elect a spokesman to do that task for them. Many of these people will be working under cover. The main one will be hidden deep into the crowd. Look for the silent one in the group while you're around and I can just about assure you that is the head of the problem.

o. They do not care about you our your family, just their own desires: The fact that you and your family may have moved across the US to serve the church there for virtually no money, you have worked as a janitor and yard man along with being a Pastor and Sunday School Teacher, all for fifty dollars a week, when they get mad at you, they don't care about you or your family. Many places have turned off utilities and even moved the minister's personal belongings into the parsonage yard and changed the door locks so they couldn't get back in and then demanded they leave. They can become ruthless and will if you don't cooperate with them in "their" plan.

p. They will quit tithing as a matter of control: They quit tithing to be able to control the Pastor's salary. If there is no money coming in, they cannot pay you long.

q. They will put their money in different places within the church to keep from having a pastor paid.

r. They will try to starve you out of the ministry

s. They will guarantee you will never pastor anywhere else again: This is my favorite. The churches act as if they control where you are sent in the ministry instead of God. Keep your head up as they tell you these things and know that they are trying to usurp their authority over God's in your calling and it will not be successful no matter how hard they try. God has you in His hand. Look in Revelation and the seven churches.

t. There are seven stars in the Right hand of Jesus. Jesus says no man can snatch you out of my hand. Pastor, you are in the loving and Mighty Hand of Jesus. He simply walks among the lamp stands and if they are not right, He removes them from Him but the Pastor is still in His right hand. Stay strong in the Lord.

u. They will verbally attack your spouse when they see no victory in attacking the minister: Yes, this will come, as they make no headway with the Pastor. They look for any place that will make the Pastor loose his or her cool. One church even accused my wife of writing my sermons for me because she was the smart one and I was too dumb to write anything. They thought they were attacking her for helping me, which she wasn't doing, but were complimenting her while they were trying to beat her down spiritually.

v. They will ultimately begin to attack your children: Our poor youngest daughter has had so many experiences in the church that at the age of 15 has written a book of her own about living in a glass walled house.

w. They will force people to take a stand and if not with them, will attack them as well: Once the battle becomes intense and they cannot succeed at getting to the minister or the Pastoral family, the people will begin to attack the people in the church that will not join in on the rally against the Pastor. This will begin to drive people out of the church and they can get the Pastoral position up for a vote and the Pastor is then gone. Once the Pastor is gone, they will find the places in the constitution that were hindrances for them and change them in the absence of a Pastor.

x. They will take every opportunity they get, from

then on, even after you leave the church to say hurtful things against you: Years down the road, these memories will still be etched into someone's mind and the lack of forgiveness will surface against you. It is no big deal, so move on with it. There are people that still have issues with me but I love them anyway.

y. They will use words like others, those people and many in confronting a situation but oftentimes it means they are not happy and that the group is really small: This group of dissenters is generally **pretty** small. They will begin to rally using words like they, them, those people, others and similar words to justify their complaint. Chances are the same lie will always come forth in that people spoke to them on the QT so they will not disclose their names. This is garbage too! The Pastor has a right to know everything and everybody that has a problem or is part of a problem. Leadership is not to be divisive but is supposed to work with the Pastor to mend problems through the proper use of scripture. People fall in one of two categories, they are either a part of the problem or part of the solution and there is no middle ground!

z. What the Lord says matters not to them as they are on their own agenda and cannot hear God anyway: Talking to them is nearly impossible to put it mildly. Their minds are made up and they will not listen to you. They are not hearing the voice of God and have no trust in Him either or they would leave the situation alone. If God wanted the Pastor to leave, God would move Him out and do a more permanent job at getting him gone than we can. They are of the belief they must do this work for God because God does these things through man. Takes us back to the book title and the explanation given by Jesus in that they know not the Father or Me! They are so reprobate that they truly believe they are doing God a service.

aa. They are in rebellion to God's Word and work: It is not you they hate. Jesus said they first hated Him. It is the spirit in you that they are rising up against. Rebellion is the very heart of the sin nature.

Ten - Look For The Victory!

1 Peter 8-11, *"Be careful! Watch out for attacks from the Devil, your great enemy. He prowls around like a roaring lion, looking for some victim to devour. Take a firm stand against him, and be strong in your faith. Remember that Christian brothers and sisters all over the world are going through the same kind of suffering you are. In His kindness, God called you to His eternal glory by means of Jesus Christ. After you have suffered a little while, he will restore, support, and strengthen you, and he will place you on a firm foundation. All power is his forever and ever, Amen."*

The Lord writes through Peter that the devil is your great enemy. The devil is not your friend! He is seeking every way that is imaginable to get a strangle hold on you and kill you. He moves around making lots of noise trying to scare you as he walks. This is the way these church people are when they get upset. They roam to and fro trying to find a way to devour you. Job says the devil is like a roaring lion with broken teeth. So what if he tries to get a hold of you. About all he can do is slobber all over you. People will look high and low to find something on you. They will reach so far back in to your past that you will wonder how they ever found that someone you have been looking for over the last twenty years. They will find people that remember you remarkably well from kindergarten class 40 years ago. These folks ought to work as private investigators for the federal government or something. It beats all I have ever seen. They will make crazy monetary commitments to take you down. These are all the devil's works. I believe if they would stop and see how ridiculous they look and sound for just one minute, they would be too embarrassed to get out into public again.

The Lord says to take a firm stand against the devil. Don't let the powerless fool push you around. The scriptures tell us to submit to the Lord, resist the devil and he shall flee. If the people knock you out of the ministry where you are, so what! God has another place for you. You have accomplished what God sent you to do. We don't seem to struggle with the open doors before us as much as we try to keep the ones behind us from closing. You may have made a mistake or two along the way but when we are truly seeking God and following what He is telling us to do, if we make a mistake, and we will, God's Grace will take care of us, as long as we were contrite in doing what was done. When we lean to our own understanding and own power and think we can conquer the devil we are surely in for a big fall. These falls may take you completely out of the ministry for a while or maybe for good. That would be God's doing at that point. Know that you have authority over the devil and that you have victory all through Christ.

The devil is so shallow in his power that he is like a small child walking up to a big 6'6" man and trying to push him. Unless the man wants to allow the baby or child to push him, he will not move. This is how we must stand in our faith. Jesus was given all power and authority and Jesus gave us His Spirit so, we've got the power, in the name of Jesus.

As ministers we are generally in one of three positions. We are either going into a critical time, in the middle of a critical time or just getting out of a critical time. There is always somebody going through what you are going through and you won't have to look far to see it. It is sad but these are the kinds of attack we Christians fall under. If we are not being attacked, we are already defeated. Through these times of struggle, there is encouragement that there is someone that would have a common understanding on what is going on and how you feel.

One of our good friends walked me through a crisis situation as we were going through it. He told me step by step what they were going to do next. It was amazing that the pattern of the devil was exactly the same. The old devil hasn't had a new trick in many years but the old ones seem to be doing ok for him. Those walking in the light of the Word will see and know where the devil is and where he is going to move next. Had it not been for this encouragement, we would surely have left the Pastoral Ministry, never to return.

God called you through Christ to come to Him and serve Him. God is going to continue to hold you in His hand as you go through times in the ministry. He has a reason that He allows these things to happen in the churches and why He chooses us to go through these with them. I don't particularly like stressful situations but if that is where God wants me, that is where I want to be. He says that after we have suffered a little while, He will restore, support and strengthen you and place you on a firm foundation. This was an awesome promise the Lord showed me after having been through a crisis in the church. Every time a situation came up and we went through it, God gave us the strength and helped us to grow through it all. God keeps us rooted in the good soil of Jesus Christ who has all power forever and ever.

Eleven - A Time of Restoration

Job 42:10-12, *"When Job prayed for his friends, the LORD restored his fortunes. In fact, the LORD gave him twice as much as before! Then all his brothers, sisters, and former friends came and feasted with him in his home. And they consoled him and comforted him because of all the trials the LORD had brought against him. And each of them brought a gift of money and a gold ring. So the LORD Blessed Job in the second half of his life even more than in the beginning."*

Job's friends left him hanging in what to do. They told him that he must have had some wrong doings somewhere or God wouldn't do the things to him that had been done. They didn't understand. When going through a church, crisis not even your family will understand, unless they have seen one before. Job was guilty of something when there was really nothing and so you will be accused as well.

Job didn't just discard his friends and get rid of them. We cannot be any different. People have no idea what you are going through or why. Many times we go through these things for no reason it appears. Sometimes we bring some things on ourselves. We cannot pretend to believe that all church crisis is a church congregation problem and Pastors are never wrong. We are wrong too from time to time. Job prayed for those that didn't understand. I imagine he was praying that God would give them understanding about his situation. I believe Job loved his friends and was hurt by their actions against him. I cannot help but to believe that Job wanted for them what He knew he had already. We do not have to be in a crisis to be praying for our friends. We should pray for people every day. We should pray even more for those that do bad things to us. God will take care of the situations around us as we pray.

After the devil ran out of tricks, the Lord restored to Job twice as much as before. If you were a mighty and powerful man of God before a crisis and the people served to drain that, how much more do you think God will use you when He restores twice as much to you? God will be glorified through it all.

Job's house was full again. It says in the scripture that Job's former friends came to his house to eat. You will have people that will stand back and maybe even talk bad about you and have nothing to do with you until the crisis is over. We were going through a crisis and we didn't have one family member come to sit in the service during any of that time to support us. They did not want to get involved and if they had, they would have been hurt too. I know not the reason they didn't come and they don't fully understand what went on. We again have some friends that had quit talking to us during a tough time that now realize we were not wrong and we are some of God's children. Job's former friends reconciled and were welcomed into his house for lunch. One day you will again eat with some of the people you may have felt betrayed you. They also come to the understanding that the trials Job had were from God and they came to speak with him.

God sent all these people in with jewelry. Ol' Job got a pay raise. He found favor with God and man. He was restored in worldly riches as well as spiritually. He was given much more than he already had. Job's marriage was restored and had children. Job received much more in the latter half of his life than he had received during the first half. He is indeed a God of Blessings and a God of Restoration!!

Blessings!

Meet the Authors
Cheryl and Randy Heddings

Cheryl (Bigelow) and Randy Heddings grew up in the same small town along the Mississippi Gulf Coast. Cheryl was raised Catholic and Randy Lutheran. Home. Cheryl learned to hear the voice of God early in life, Randy later.

Cheryl and Randy met, married, and raised four children. When their third child graduated from high school, Cheryl and Randy realized they were called to Christian ministry.

Cheryl, Randy, and Jessica (twelve-year old daughter) went to central Texas to start new works. They went with no money, no demographic facts, and no church planting training. For the next two years they served God and followed His will only. In response, the Holy Spirit amazed them with His guidance of their ministry.